Wedding M
for
Solo Violin

by Katherine Curatolo

Visit … ***ail@melbay.com***

Introduction

Written for solo violin without need for piano accompaniment, this collection contains straightforward arrangements of the selections most frequently requested for wedding ceremonies. Inside you will find traditional wedding favorites as well as beautiful classical pieces to create an elegant musical experience. The pieces are loosely grouped according to their traditional or suggested usage: prelude music, processionals, music for the ceremony, and recessionals. These labels are fluid, and songs can be used in various ways as a part of the wedding ceremony.

Table of Contents

Air from *Water Music* .... G. F. Handel 4
Air on the G String .... J. S. Bach 23
Allegro from *The Four Seasons–Spring* .... A. Vivaldi 10
Arioso .... J. S. Bach 6
Ash Grove, The 5
Ave Maria .... F. Schubert 20
Ave Verum Corpus .... W. A. Mozart 24
Bist du bei mir .... G. H. Stölzel 22
Bridal Chorus from *Lohengrin* .... R. Wagner 18
Canon in D .... J. Pachelbel 14
Hornpipe from *Water Music* .... G. F. Handel 30
Intermezzo from *Cavelleria Rusticana* .... P. Mascagni 16
Jesu, Joy of Man's Desiring .... J. S. Bach 12
La Rejouissance .... G. F. Handel 31
Largo from *The Four Seasons-Winter* .... A. Vivaldi 9
Largo from *Xerxes* .... G. F. Handel 25
Ode to Joy .... L. van Beethoven 7
Rondeau .... J. Mouret 29
Sheep May Safely Graze .... J. S. Bach 8
Trumpet Tune .... H. Purcell 28
Trumpet Voluntary .... J. Clarke 17
Wachet auf (Sleepers Awake) .... J. S. Bach 26
Wedding March .... F. Mendelssohn 27

Air

from *Water Music*

George Frideric Handel
Arranged K. Curatolo

The Ash Grove

Traditional
Arranged K. Curatolo

Arioso

Johann Sebastian Bach
Arranged K. Curatolo

Ode to Joy

Ludwig van Beethoven
Arranged K. Curatolo

Sheep May Safely Graze

from *Cantata No. 208*

Johann Sebastian Bach
Arranged K. Curatolo

Largo

from *The Four Seasons–Winter*

Antonio Vivaldi
Arranged K. Curatolo

Allegro

from *The Four Seasons–Spring*

Antonio Vivaldi
Arranged K. Curatolo

rit.

Jesu, Joy of Man's Desiring

Johann Sebastian Bach
Arranged K. Curatolo

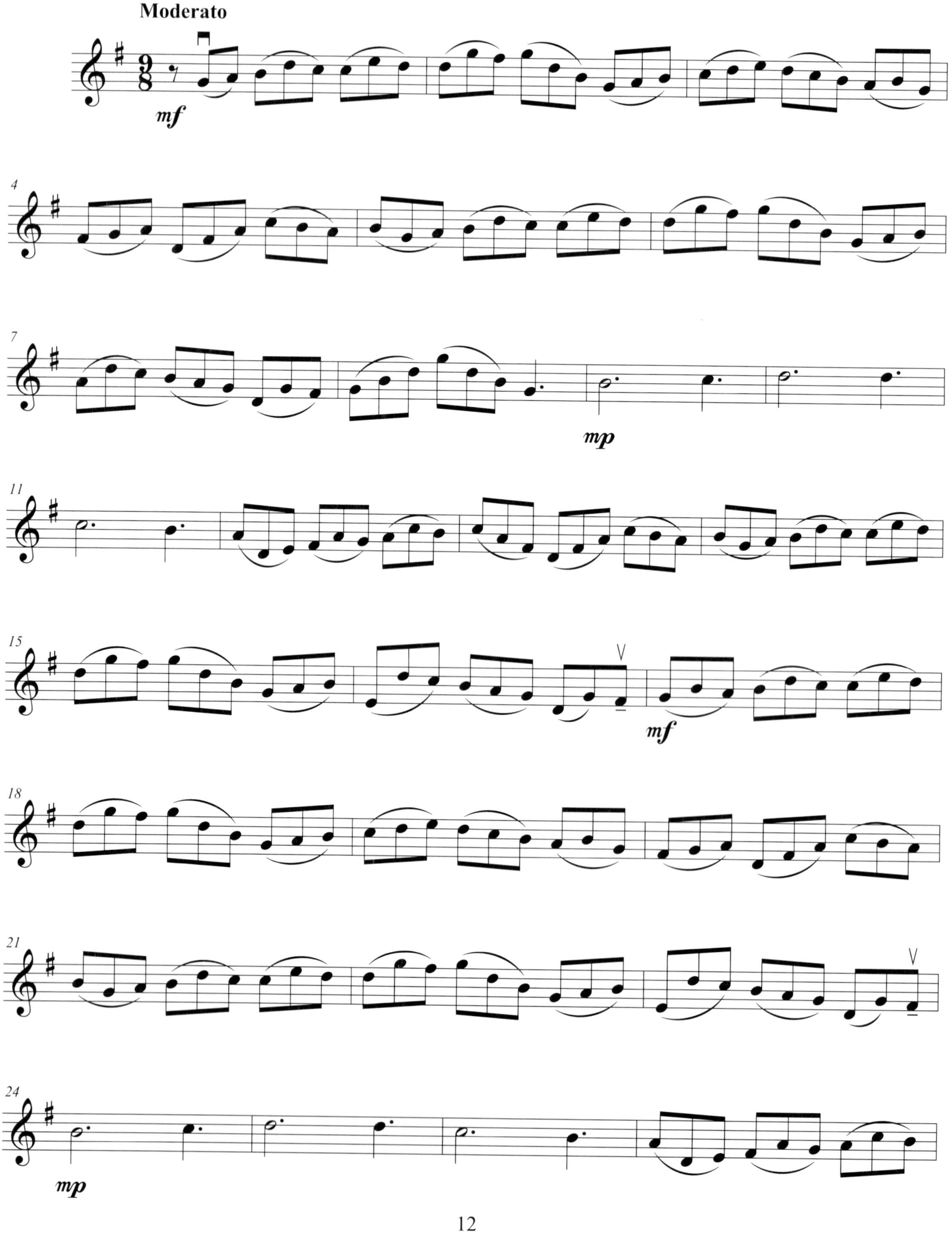

28
mf
31
f
34
37
rit.

Canon in D

Johann Pachelbel
Arranged K. Curatolo

21
24
27
29
32
tr
35
39
rit.

Intermezzo
from *Cavelleria Rusticana*

Pietro Mascagni
Arranged K. Curatolo

Trumpet Voluntary

Jeremiah Clarke
Arranged K. Curatolo

Bridal Chorus

from *Lohengrin*

Richard Wagner
Arranged K. Curatolo

41
46
51
55
59

Ave Maria

Franz Schubert
Arranged K. Curatolo

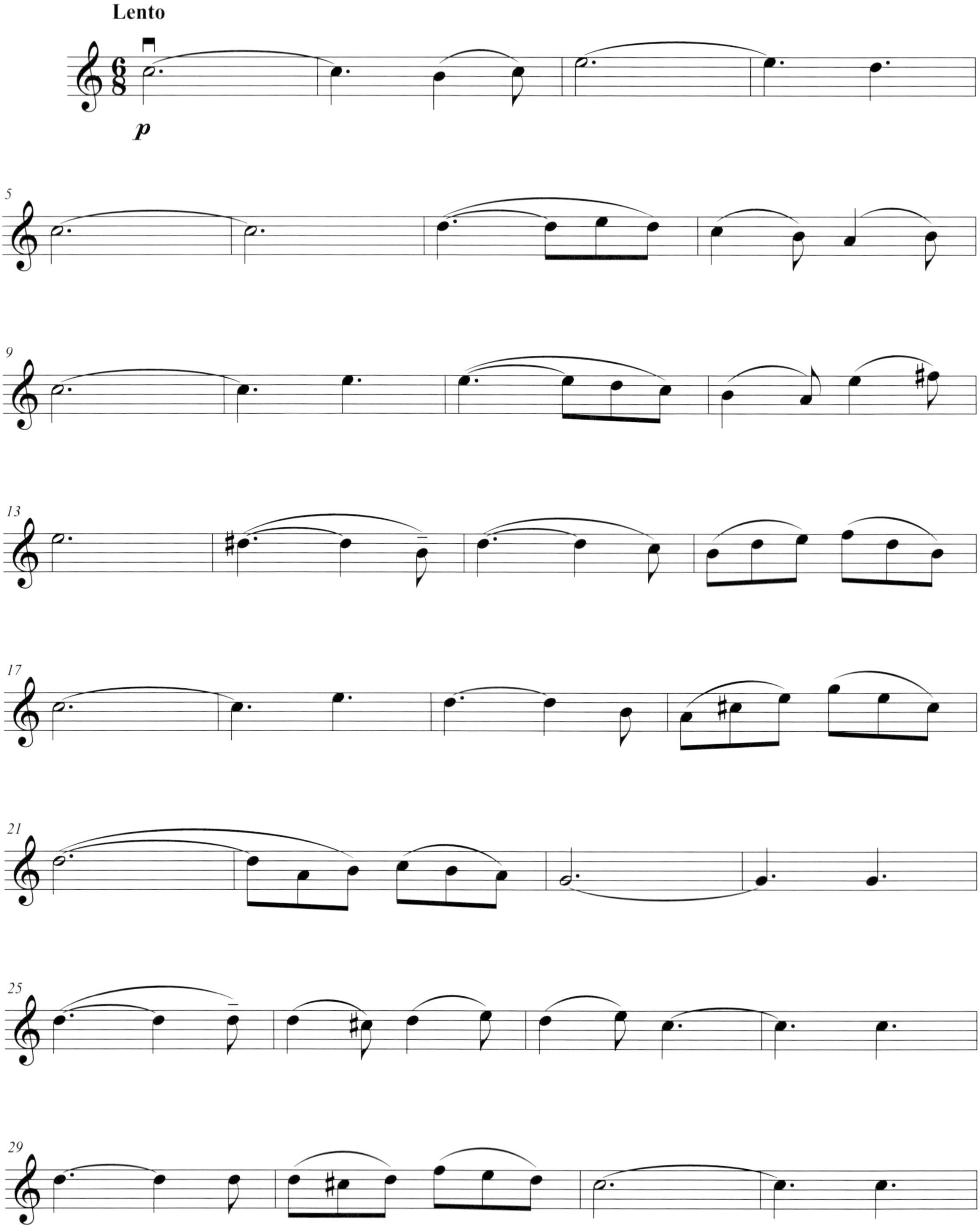

33
mf
37
41
p
46
rit.

Bist du bei mir

Gottfried Heinrich Stölzel
Arranged K. Curatolo

Air on the G String

Johann Sebastian Bach
Arranged K. Curatolo

Ave Verum Corpus

Wolfgang Amadeus Mozart
Arranged K. Curatolo

Largo
from *Xerxes*

George Frideric Handel
Arranged K. Curatolo

Wachet auf
(Sleepers Awake)

Johann Sebastian Bach
Arranged K. Curatolo

Wedding March

from *A Midsummer Night's Dream*

Felix Mendelssohn
Arranged K. Curatolo

Trumpet Tune

Henry Purcell
Arranged K. Curatolo

Rondeau

Jean–Joseph Mouret
Arranged K. Curatolo

Hornpipe
from *Water Music*

George Frideric Handel
Arranged K. Curatolo

La Rejouissance

George Frideric Handel
Arranged K. Curatolo

MEL BAY®